Heinz Henghes

The sculptor Heinz Henghes was born in Hamburg in 1906. He first took up sculpture as a young man in America thanks to the influence of Noguchi. Returning to Europe he met many artists, notably Brancusi, along with writers including Henry Miller, Jean Genet and Anais Nin who wrote of him in her Journals. In Italy Ezra Pound became his patron and he exhibited with Kay Sage whom he was to introduce to her future husband Yves Tanguy. In England he initially exhibited at the Guggenheim Jeune gallery. He wrote extensively on current affairs and art for the BBC as well as writing stories, poetry, wide-ranging articles and a play. After the war he taught at the Royal College of Art, and took part in shows including Sculpture in the Home and the Festival of Britain. He moved to set up his studio in the Dordogne whilst holding solo exhibitions internationally, before returning to England to become head of the sculpture school at the Winchester School of Art. He died in France in 1975.

More information and links relating to this book, along with a chronology and a catalogue of works, can be found at **www.henghes.org**

Ecce Ego
The First Thing

HEINZ HENGHES

Eothea

www.eothea.com
www.henghes.org

Published by Eothea 2006

'The First Thing' was first published in 1953 in the U.S.A. by
New Directions - New Directions in Prose and Poetry No. 14.

ISBN-13: 978-0-9552566-0-8
ISBN-10: 0-9552566-0-7

Printed and bound in Great Britain
By CPI London

Eothea
92 Highgate Hill
London N6 5HE
Great Britain

For Katerina di San Faustino
(Kay Sage 1898 - 1963)

Introduction

1939 found Heinz Henghes living at No 3 Cavaye Studios off the Fulham Road in London. He had arrived in England two years before, a young sculptor who had already spent time in Paris with Brancusi and lived, worked and exhibited for some years in Italy, where his first patron was Ezra Pound.

The outbreak of war was a particular anxiety for Heinz. He was at the time a German national with a Jewish mother and Lutheran father. His parents lived in Germany though he had seen neither of them for many years. He had adopted 'Henghes' as an alias to use as an artist, his papers bore the name Gustav Heinrich Clusmann. Following the outbreak of war there was much suspicion in England of foreigners, especially Germans. The papers started stories about '5th columnists'. These were supposedly infiltrators bent on sabotaging the national infrastructure and spying for the enemy. Industrial accidents were blamed on them and according to certain sections of the media they could easily be disguised SS men. The reaction to this from politicians was to 'Collar the Lot', as Churchill put it. Within a few months this climate of fear was to lead to Heinz being interned and sent to Australia with some 2,500 other men on the transport ship the 'Dunera'. The voyage was to become notorious for the ill treatment the internees suffered at the hands of the British soldiers guarding them. The British Governments policy on internment had been hastily implemented and was in a state of flux. Even before they reached their ultimate destination, an internment camp at

Hay in New South Wales, the policy regarding 'enemy aliens' had been considerably softened. Many still in the U.K. were never arrested. Not long after it was decided that those already interned who were deemed to present no risk were to be released. Despite this the Australians were not disposed to set them free so they were kept imprisoned. Heinz was one of the lucky ones, and with help from supporters in England including Herbert Read was amongst the first to return in 1941. For the rest of the war he was to work in London for the BBC writing on current affairs, and as an Air Raid Protection warden. After the war he adopted British nationality and changed his name by deed poll to Henry Henghes.

At the end of 1939 Heinz could not be sure of his wartime fate, but the stress he felt was at times considerable. He had recently written for the 'Adelphi' magazine, a journal concerned with the cause of peace, about the importance of Americas relationship to Europe and the inevitability of greater European integration in a changing world economy, through either peaceful or forced means.

The young Joan Wyndham met Heinz at this time and gives a vivid portrait of him in her book 'Love Lessons: A Wartime Diary' in which she names him 'Gehardt'. It is clear that Heinz believed his future to be bleak. He knew that it was likely he would be interned by the British, but should the Germans invade he thought he would be shot as a traitor. Perhaps as an escape from present troubles he wrote an account of his life in New York and of meeting the girl who was to become his first wife. Joan, on reading a draft manuscript at the time commented in her diary: 'If

Heinz wants to keep hidden behind his barriers of cynicism he really shouldn't write such revealing books'.

Some fifteen years earlier, on the 21st June 1924 Heinz left his native Hamburg for America, stowing away on board the 'Deutschland', a passenger ship bound for New York. U.S. records show him on arrival listed as the ships boy. A few days after the initial entry, he appears in the official record again, this time as a 'deserting seaman'. The Deutschland was to sail home without him.

Alone in New York, a 17 year-old Heinz found himself in Central Park uncertain of his future. An old lady sat down next to him and said 'hello' but quickly realised he knew next to no English. They managed to communicate as Heinz knew some words of Yiddish, and it was thanks to this encounter that he got a job washing dishes.

Heinz was virtually destitute when he was first in New York, knowing the reality of an 'empty belly'. To still hunger pangs he would drink water from public fountains, or if he had a little money take a cup of coffee and empty the sugar bowl into his pockets to eke out the sweetness during the day. After a while his mother managed to contact Heinz through Interpol, and for a time sent him a small allowance which helped him to live. As well as washing dishes Heinz learned how to make pancakes and got some work loading cargo at the New York docks. This was the age of Prohibition, though the law banning the sale of alcohol was proving largely unenforceable.

Quickly picking up English Heinz lived by his wits. Soon he would get food from café owners who came to know him for his ability to engage in conversation and saw in him a handsome young man whose presence might be good for trade. To be able to join in intellectual debates and hold his own Heinz would go to the library whenever a subject was discussed that he knew little about, and thus he continued his self-education, gaining an eclectic mix of knowledge in philosophy, the arts and sciences. Self-reliance was something that Heinz was keen to foster in his students in later years, saying they did not realize what an easy life they had.

'Ecce Ego - The First Thing' is only half the story, the second part set in London, is not published in this volume. In it there is a section recollecting his early life in New York that clearly pre-dates the rest of the work and so is worth reproducing here. It gives a particular insight on the harsher part of his life in New York and the impact the city had on the young man from Hamburg discovering his interest in sculpture.

> *Funny, guess it'll be the same all my life, sculpture, modern at that, such an impractical art, might at least have picked on painting, people like pretty baubles of colour, hate to be a guy tickling a canvas with a brush though, sissy amusement, not like stone, granite, tough as iron, tougher, and a big hammer. How the steel rings. It's like New York, not quite as bad, thank God, but on the edge of it, used to sleep in the subway, sneak under the turnstyle at night and ride back and forth from the Bronx to Coney Island, two hour ride, cold and they kick you out in Coney Island while they clean the trains. Railroad cops give you hard stares, never bothered me though guess they saw I was harmless, too dopey to steal. Old men try to pick you up sometimes, pinch you and make furtive*

grabs for you in the crowd, loose, senile lips,- that is horrible, but it went right over my head, one gets so crude and calloused that those things seem funny, just made me laugh, should have cried, I suppose, only you don't get much time to cry. Hocked my jacket for 25 cents, to live on Woolworth candy, pound for 5 cents, lived on that, sugar, glucose, energy, ruined my teeth though, I did need my overcoat, though that would have brought more, 50 cents if the guy was kind-hearted, only they never are. But I couldn't hock that because I had to look for jobs with an overcoat on, respectable, sort of. Restaurant jobs as dishwasher or busboy, 72 Dollars a week, 12 hours a day, or maybe night work, couldn't get anything else because at least they feed you. Give you a white jacket, they do, couldn't have held out on another job, on nothing and no place to sleep. Dirty bastards, night managers, work you to death in stinking kitchens, always full of cockroaches, enormous beasts the American brand, red with wings, quite harmless though, just eat garbage. Well, how I did it I don't know, funny the underground life that goes on in the subway.... In the wintertime they light stoves in the waiting rooms and if the ticketagent had had a good dinner you could go to sleep behind them for an hour or so. Slept so soundly once after two days without rest that my leg fell against the stove and got a long burn, still got the scar, and I never felt it burn. And even at that, all that was a graduation, a step up from the sweatshop on Canal street, shirt factory, and 8 Dollars a week and no food and docked if you were ten minutes late and they all but beat you to make you work faster, faster and if you ruined a piece of cloth you paid for it, If you cut your thumb off on their machine they called it carelessness. How was it again? The strange ways of destiny,-picked up on the street I was by that young man, asking me to come and pose for him and I thought 'fairy' and didn't go, and then meeting him a second time, only this time he was with a girl and I liked her looks and so I went. He was a sculptor and watching him work I began to play with clay. Thought it was wonderful, the first thing I made, silly little figure with a hoop in her arms, must have been all distorted, though that wouldn't matter much if it had hung together, but it didn't, but that man he sent me to was kind... Enormous Italian, hands and shoulders like an ox, Michaelangelo type, maestro and here was I, new disciple, so he tore my little statue to bits and I hated him for it, but on the chance of his word my whole future hung at that moment, What if he's merely said 'No good, get out.' Old Marelli, and so many people have been Kind to me. Soon it'll be my turn to be kind to these young things without an idea who are nothing but an inflated ego, but the germ hides in that and I must remember.

Heinz lived for a time at No 3 University Place. The Japanese-American sculptor Noguchi had just set up a studio at Number 127 and was to be a great influence on Heinz. From modelling and assisting Noguchi Heinz took up sculpture himself and Noguchi was to be his critic. Heinz reminded Noguchi of Gaudia-Brzeska as portrayed in 'Savage Messiah' and he told him as much.

Heinz met many artists and writers during his time in New York and began to write himself. Some published poetry of his gained the attention of Ezra Pound, who wrote to him saying that he should come and see him if he came to Italy. A few years later Heinz was to follow up this invitation and Pound was to house him and help him considerably as he started to carve stone.

By 1929 Heinz had done enough work to be exhibited at different galleries including Marie Sterner, International, Downtown, and Weyhe. His first one-man show was to come at the Friends of Art, Baltimore a couple of years later.

At around this time Heinz fell in love with Mary Elizabeth Crabtree, the 'Betty' of 'Ecce Ego'. On January 1st 1931 they married in Rockville, Maryland. She was 19 and he 24. The newly-weds lived in New York in an apartment the young bride, now pregnant, said she found 'cold' and 'un-liveable'. With cracks fast appearing in the marriage the couple moved to Washington to be near Mary's family. Her unhappiness deepened and Heinz became depressed. Mary left for Cincinnati to have her baby. By January 1932 Mary wanted a divorce and travelled to Reno, as Nevada was a state where quick divorces were to be obtained. Heinz followed her there on the 9th February. Two days later he was admitted to the Nevada State Hospital suffering from 'acute insanity' brought on by depression following an argument with his wife and an attempted suicide using poison. The divorce was granted. Soon after this the FBI approached Heinz who was an 'illegal' in the country as his status had never been regularised since he jumped ship some 8 years earlier. He was persuaded to return to Europe.

'Ecce Ego - The First Thing' is written as an autobiographical novella. In it Heinz adopts the alias 'Dick' and gives us a rich insight into his impressions of New York. It was first published in 1953 by New Directions. This is the first edition to include the artists original illustrations.

An appendix accompanying this edition contains background material cross-referenced to the text. Additional information and links may be found at:
www.henghes.org/ecceego

Ecce Ego
The First Thing

New York 1930

The first thing that attracted her to him was that he person-ified her own, unphrased desire for freedom. The being without ties, without family and therefore without respon-sibility. The unkemptness and not caring that meant free-dom to her emerging mind. The first thing that attracted her to him was that he did not kiss her at once while they were alone in the square, cement walled room in which all the students worked three hours a day, that he did not try to put his hand on her left breast, embracing her, as the others had done, as seemed to her to be the formula of the game love. The first thing that attracted her to him was that an unconscious rapport seemed to exist between them that drew them naturally into each other's company, into an understanding that was wordless and found words in their expressions of solidarity against the other students. The best places near the model, the most malleable clay, the most solid modelling stands. They were the strongest among the ten students in this bare room, and they shared their strength and tried it on each other.

After the first ten days of their acquaintance, as they lay, their nude bodies fallen away from each other on the small bed of her room, she ceased to think about him. He became part of the half-somnolent dream in her head of which she constructed her life, and her consciousness of him stirred and flickered and sometimes awoke painfully only in the degree in which he stepped outside that dream, disrupting its easy flow. And this she thought of as hurt.

The matter of which this dream had grown was the hodgepodge of conflict that had imposed itself upon her. The dimly felt realities of life that had come her way had little part in the complexity of her conclusions. Her parents believed in kindness and in right. Children were to be guided and their aberrations from the fixed norm were corrected gently and with superior assurance. (Mother knows best, dear - the tone of voice tired and correctly soothing.) The necessity to correct (part of the cross we all must bear) was never a thing that her parents thought of as mutable. Their values were too proven for that. Proof is what shields and protects, and we want our daughter to lead a sheltered and secure life when she grows up and to have a good husband.

Under the gentle influence of this dulcet eunuch choir she had been lulled into the warm protection of a cocoon in which she was safe. The outer world got through to her only after an elaborate process of decontamination and filtration which stripped it of its nasty verities and gave it a mother-of-pearl sheen. But if her parents had thought of giving her a system that would guard her against the hostilities of life, a system based on the principles of combat and the right answers to situation X, they had not thought of the nefarious quality of nature. They had not thought of the biological machine with its deep and terrible roots that suck nastily inside the blood. They had never dreamt of life as an insatiable thing that began as an avid parasite in the womb.

She had been a late child. Conceived when her parents were already ageing she had been what is known as a blessing and (with two growing daughters already in the house) a somewhat naughty thing. What will the girls think, their eyes solemn and looking. They know. You can feel their looks like tangible shafts of crawling curiosity going into me - and the mother had retracted her belly with each fancied look and had spoken sweetly to the two girls who

did know and pretended not to notice and lived in a delighted state of titillated wonder. Run along now children
and play.

And the blind grinning and sardonic embryo inside,
rooted to the wall of her womb and extending groping
invisible tendrils into her bloodstream and into her brain
and the marrow of her bones and her spinal column had felt
her feelings and had felt each look, and tied as it was to the
inner things and unconscious of the right and the just and
the Christian and the time-honoured answers, the shivers
that went over its mother's belly had hit straight home and
became sex. And in time it grew and swelled, lost gills and
tail, developed and was born - a sweet little baby. Come and
see your baby sister, girls ... Mustn't bother mother with
questions now ... God gave her to us. Her name was Betty.

The dream was in itself conflict. Built of the sense of
the right to be sheltered and the fear of the unknown, mixed
with the dark curiosity of sex and the drive to match forces
against the ancient phallic things to see who would prevail,
it made her into a streamlined modern version of a nymph
on a Grecian Urn, dancing perpetually around the tree of
life and running from fauns to fall into the simple-minded
traps of casual satyrs.

But they knew nothing of this this warm afternoon
on her bed. They had slipped into their embrace with an
ease and a naturalness which was unknown to both of
them. There had been no strife and no conquest, no arched
back and glittering eyes. It had happened and this it-had-
happened, happened somehow without them, appalled
them now. A frantic narcissism had taken hold of them and
they lay beside one another each alone, regarding avidly his

own body and stroking each his own thighs and belly and chest, trying to reconquer themselves, trying to rediscover their own body as an independent thing, free, a unit existant only for the sake of self and not as part of something too vast flown together. Their minds shied from the thing in which a moment ago they had been swept into forgetting to watch, forgetting to derive an identifiable I-won articulation, the thing in which they had found themselves sucked into something that they did not know and that was a vortex which knew no thought nor sensing but made them, made their bodies, into the floating, impersonal and vast sense Itself.

There had been no conquest, no feather in my cap, they had been possessed by a thing and had themselves become that thing. But their astonished fear sank back again and submerged under their caressing hands which strayed and slipped to a breast and around back, spine; legs touching, shivering turn to each other and thighs spreading - how warm you are, and lost ...

Walking home, the usual cat that licked the cream feeling would not come to him. He felt easeful and relaxed, as though a soft palm had smoothed down all the nerve-ends in his body and strangely, unfamiliarly, the life around him did not seem hostile, something to match one's wits against now. The street lights cast a pattern through the foliage of trees whose leaves were now, just before autumn, fat and gleaming. People sat on the benches overlooking the river, lost in the beauty of the strong lights of the Palisades on the opposite shore and a little boat with green eyes on the shimmering water. Downtown stood the stark silhouette of the immense glistening skyscrapers. There was no

Her name was Betty

sky. All the exuberant force of New York blazed upward and outlined only itself, effacing the stars. Tonight, somehow, there was cohesion in all this. It hung together. It clicked; and flown together it had become comprehensive and human. For a single moment the city and he spoke to one another with humor and tolerance and grace. "Lick me ... I hope you can ..." "And if I can't, it'll be fun trying." The compact mob on Broadway was co-related tonight. It had a unity of sense which made him see it for the first time in his life as a single thing. All these people, struggling and pushing and milling around, as though aimlessly, were interconnected by an invisible string of common being. They were not lives, but life and the ambitions of one fitted into the needs of others. Their senses complemented one another. It was a strange world without edges and corners. Many leaves on a stem.

Like an unending vibration of a deep-toned string, a current of common being hummed through him. The single spectacle of existence lay open to him, the spectacle of the transient being, fearfully obsessed by the thought of I, but possessed by the vaster thing, the belonging together, the inseparability from the silent and mysterious growth underneath. It made sense, the striving. The newsboy made sense - "Read all about it, moider in Queens!" The fat man with the cigar, shoving people out of his preoccupied way ... the blonde with a smile fixed by hard glittering habit ... the angry policeman directing howling, impatient cars ... the bootblacks ... the young clerks and their girls ... the bitter shopgirls with their eyes seeking for unspoken insults ... all the waste and confusion, the self-seeking determination made sense after all. It was all going some place, rolling, milling along without apparent direction, but the milling was the seething germination within the vast drift of time. Something compacted these beings on Broadway, all over the city and in the entire world into a coherent thing that depended on its cohesion. They needed each other and out of that need and all unheeded grew their splendid simplicities. "An atom in the stream," he thought. But the phrase destroyed his comprehension. It became at once conditional. The inevitable "And the I is the interpreter of me," added itself naturally, through the habit of countless generations of seeking to understand - and to understand is to phrase.

The illuminated clock of the Metropolitan Life Building hung suspended in the sky. The tower black and lightless. 10:30 plenty of time to go to Paul's. Things will just be getting hot there. Past the Flatiron Building, down Fifth Avenue, the overflow of the garment trade, fashionable address but tawdry all the same and up 8th Street. There it is. The doorman has a set of buttons behind him that he can lean against; they flash green, red or yellow inside. Green is O.K., red is cop and yellow means tough guy. The tough guys are little tinhorn gangsters trying to horn in, trying to get a liquor concession and saying: "You better do it or else ... you know what happens to guys that wont play." Truth is, they've been to the movies too often. The cops try all sorts of tricks because Paul is a good upstanding citizen and refuses to pay graft. Why should he when they have to catch him first and then maybe it'll only mean a fine? So the cops put on a regular show almost every night, first a harness bull, saying the neighbors are complaining, too much noise and you better stop it or else we'll take away your license from you. Then maybe a couple of plainclothes dicks, vice squad, city health bureau, fire department, anything they can think of. Dress themselves up swell to look like suckers from uptown, screaming to be taken for their roll, or maybe come around looking like stew bums or, one night, dressed up as artists, big portfolio under their arm and open, dirty collar. But the doorman has a nose for cops like a terrapin hound and anyway he doesn't trust strange faces nor two men together without girls and so all the bottles have disappeared under the tables by the time they get in and the music has stopped and maybe there is some nut up there reciting poetry. "Between my toes a dainty lace-work spreads ..."

The place is jammed to the doors, six and eight crowded together at small tables and squeezed in a compact row, like sparrows on a fence in winter, all along the benches that run around the walls. A smoke cloud hangs over the long room, dense as fog and the waitresses rush around trying to do their best. These waitresses are hand picked by the boss himself, good color hair, neat figure, pretty, and to each he has given an elaborate set of instructions. No picking up customers, girls, or else you're fired. And he has invented a horrible tale about how one of his waitresses was railroaded to jail for six months by the vice squad, to frighten them. And no accepting bills for tips, might be marked money. If a drunk looks as though he wants to get tough, tip me off and no sneaking sandwiches to the Village bums unless I say it's O.K.

The Village bums were a fixture and an attraction of the place. The suckers come to Greenwich Village for an arty atmosphere and they know damn well what an arty atmosphere should be like so we'll give it to them. No need to dress the boys up, they look the part naturally - dirty clothes, no ties, long hair and that slouch; even when they sit down they look as though they never had a nickel and dont care. We'll have a symposium one night, Mondays maybe, slack day, subject "Why women?" - plenty hot that, maybe pep things up a bit. And Tuesday and Friday, poetry night. Make 'em recite; three poems and then turn on the gramophone for twenty minutes and let 'em dance before the next poet comes on. Beauty contest on Wednesday, the customers judge, applause and lewd cracks; something lively going on every evening.

The Villagers were an exclusive set, snooty as the hoi-polloi, always sat at a large table near the end of the room, fourteen, sixteen together and outsiders didn't have a chance. The gang just froze up if anybody tried to horn in, or else they'd tear the guy to bits, use five syllable words on him and ask nasty questions: what did he think of relativity and how about the Apollonic counterpoint to the Dionysian flux?[1] Their table was their table and let the guys from uptown go sit someplace else, all over the room, but not here. Maybe they'd walk over sooner or later and get a drink or something off them, but not among us. They hung together tenaciously and in their tenacity lay their means of protection against a hostile and uncomprehending world. Alone they would have collapsed before the implied jealous sneer that lay in the approach of these outsiders and in their curiosity. "Well, a poet, that's O.K., but why dont you get a job?" But together they were safe. Their unruly asocial instinct was fortified by the mass. They were truly poor and of an incredible courage. None had proven himself. They had nothing but their ego that told them, "I am it." Nothing but their ego and their merciless comradeship.

"We Garrities have always been court jesters to the kings of Ireland," says Johnny in his high, squeaky voice. "Poets we were." And he has to lift his water glass which is half filled with gin with both hands, they tremble so. Been on another one of his terrible binges for the last two weeks, he has. He drinks incredibly and his periods of sobriety are no more than brief interludes between drunks, enforced by waking up in a police cell or by a physical breakdown. Dypsomaniac, and sometimes he has visions and sees things that come for him and he screams and throws himself about and has to be held down. Or else persecution mania. Liable to turn on you and say very gently and with great sweetness, "Why do you want to do it? Why do you want to kill me?"

"The bastard, the god-damn bastard," Lionel thinks, "found him last night out cold in front of my door, God knows how he got into the house, and I dragged him inside and put him to bed unconscious and he pissed in the bed and woke up chipper as anything this morning ... how does he do it, year after year, and here he is crowing and ranting, off on another one." If you turn your head away Johnny will snatch your glass quick. A little trick he developed and it raises a laugh sometimes, but he shouldn't do it to his pals, hard enough it is to scrounge drinks. The glasses within Johnnie's reach are held firmly in the hands of their owners. He is wearing a checked shirt with a black string tie which is tightly knotted below the open collar and someone's discarded polo coat. The coat is far too large for him. With each motion his hands disappear in the sleeves, but he is aware

I am it.

of the comic value of his costume and uses the long sleeves for elaborate and accentuated gestures, flapping them about and hunching his shoulders to make his ears disappear inside the frayed collar. His head rolls back and he blows out his cheeks. The court jester, the lineage of the kings of Ireland mysteriously interwoven in his blood - of course they crept into Milady's chamber at night, a buxom wench under the greenwood tree and his majesty's trumpeters heralding the approach of the king, the jester, the jesterking, the king-jester from the battlements. A hale and hearty fellow, a toss-pot with the best of them, a Falstaff and a Henry of England, but Hamlet too, all in a polo coat with sleeves too long for his thin arms.

His sinister friend, the mad painter, bays like a dog by way of laughter and someone strikes up a derisive chant - a toast unto his Majesty - which Johnny takes standing, as a salute. Jake, who has lately discovered Kant sits by himself in the midst of the turmoil, reading and moving his lips with each word he reads after the manner of the Jews. He has found a sentence which enchants and delights him and which he keeps reading over and over again until it becomes audible of itself. "Christ," he says, "Listen to this: `according to the bare concept, the inner is the substratum of all conditions or outer determinations ...' "

They listen. They listen aggressively and determined to contradict and refute. "Nuts," says Lionel, "there is no bare concept and conditions are the determining factor of our existence ..." He has bitten off the whole thing, almost without thinking, but Jake is pained.

"You don't get it," and he reads the sentence again.

"Yeah, well," But no one can take the word from Jake now. "Don't you see, it fits right in with Freud and even with Watson,[2] don't you see ..."

And these two fashionable names strike the right key. They are names that pull the rabbit out of the hat, names that carry their own assurance and bring the beautiful vista of unending technical terms right smack to your own front door.

"Sure, I see," Lionel, eager, interrupts, "You mean the inner as the libidino and various forms of complexes being the substratum of extravert manifestations, but I don't see Watson, I don't see Behaviourist concepts in it. They say just the opposite, the determinate acting on the indeterminate."

"Oh, Jeesus," says Jake, "What'd I ever start it for, lemme explain, see ..."

But each thinks his own thoughts, the words of the other, half-heard and unexamined, pass through their minds as small rumblings that have no continuity. The issue is already fixed and decided. You can't tell me anything, I know, let me find out for myself ...

The roar of Vachel Lindsay's "Jungle"[3] comes from the floor. Eli is at it again. "Fat black bucks in a wine-barrel room." Each word is thrown out explosively and sharp and he roars with the lines and gesticulates, whines and snarls, his eyes tight shut and his body contorting and tense. Some wit once called in the cops while Eli was doing his act, said there was a riot in the joint and they dragged off Eli saying he must be nuts. He kept screaming, "It's a poem, I'm reciting a poem ..."

Pretty as a picture postcard, Patricia powders, pit, pat, fluff fluff, her nose. In the circle of the elect the queen is still king and Joe watches her every movement, his jutting beard quivering with each pat. Pink downy fuzz clings to her cheek and she brushes it away impatiently with a delicate and impervious gesture. Pollen on the lily. Pitty pat goes Patricia and Joe feels pitty pat on her behind, on her pink round behind, but he knows he'll never get there and cackles, the nanny goat snicker of the satirist. He begins to sing a derisive chant:

> Molly McGuire had a ping pong ball
> Round and smooth and white and all
> and she used to throw it up
> and she used to let it fall,
> Molly McGuire and her ping pong ball.

The gang delighted and at once sensing the spirit of the thing, takes it up:

> Molly McGuire had a pussy cat
> Soft and smooth and you know what
> and she used to take it round
> and she used to let it scat,
> Molly McGuire and her pussy cat.

But they make too much noise and are told to shut up: "Want to have the cops down on us?" Or else, get the hell out, and they shut up quick. Someone has given Johnny a bottle of bath tub gin and he has quickly gulped down half of it before the raven had a chance to descend on him. Now he is good and drunk and getting sore at the racket and the stink of it all and something within him is hurt and insulted. He is running around the room screeching petulantly that everybody is a lot of bastards and he is a poet and he writes his poems for the stinking lot of them who can all go to hell. Poor Johnny who has been lonely all his life. When he gets near the door the boss sees his chance to get him out with a minimum of bother and grabbing him by the scruff of the neck and the seat of his torn pants runs him through the door, but not without a louder wail of "bastard" and on outraged "let me go!" Johnny clatters around the entrance, but the doorman won't let him in again. He'll be back to-morrow, sober, and no one will say a word about it. It's all in the game and part of the fun. At the table they hardly pay any attention; might happen to any of us, better not to look. Only I wouldn't come back, each thinks; but how could they stay away? The enormous city around them, the whole continent, is reduced for them to a few streets in which they find something that they themselves can only define as a state of mind, without which they would disappear, swal-lowed by the weight of the norm which would overwhelm each in his own way.

Johnny is still waiting when they get out. He ap-pears out of a hallway where he has been dozing. It is cold and he has become a little sobered from freezing in his thin clothes. "Anybody got a place to sleep for me?" he asks. He never has a place of his own, never had one except two years ago when someone gave him a cool hundred and fifty bucks to publish some stuff with and he hired an apartment for a week with twenty, painted one room black and sat in it and drank up the rest of the dough in five days. Dick says, "O.K., but you can't stay all day; I'm gonna kick you out about noon, when I get up, and want to do some work." Johnny promises reassuringly that he has an appointment uptown anyhow and has to get up at eleven, collect some dough. But it's a convention, this uptown, and he'll sleep all day.

The girl Betty does not recur in Dick's thoughts. He does not think: I love her, nor does he seek to explain her and what happened, in his mind. He does not think: what now?, because life has no continuity and no pattern in his world. Situations loom as unrelated objects out of the outer fog that surrounds his being and enter more or less into the inner circle of light of which he is the center, but this circle is really a travelling sphere which surrounds him completely. A sphere which is constantly drifting along in an unknown space pushed by an unperceived mind and what happens to him is what the sphere encounters and engulfs for a while until it sinks back and becomes past. As though situations were unexpected objects fixed in time to which his sphere rolls up engulfing them for a moment to leave them behind again still fixed where they had been since ages ago, waiting. A few things though are carried by the impetus. Perhaps they were not firmly rooted to their position in time and get torn loose, swallowed and absorbed, unnoticed. But they set up a sinister metabolism within the sphere, a chemical process which is imperceptible to him. They are the bacillae of the creeping disease, growth. He will see Betty again tomorrow, walking into the plain gray room. He will be neither early nor late, just in his own time. She will wear the same dress and her hair will not be done differently for him. Perhaps they will have lunch together - tomato soup out of a tin and crackers out of a box, malted milk with ice-cream at the drug store and cigarettes.

Johnny, by his side, is shaking with cold. He has a mild attack of the horrors. "Jesus," he says, "Got the shivers, got them bad, two quarts of gin, Jesus, can't stop shaking." And he groans in fear.

They climb into the rickety bed together and lie between the grimy sheets with a last cigarette. Johnny, getting warm, falls asleep almost at once, exhausted, but Dick lies awake yet awhile thinking of the bedbugs. Nothing you can do about them. Move the bed away from the wall and they climb up anyway; put the legs in tins of kerosene and you'll probably set yourself on fire. The bedbugs will climb up to the ceiling and drop straight down on you, cunning bastards. The whole house is infested with them, the whole quarter, too old. But it seems that you get immune to them after a while, at least to your own kind, the ones that have been biting you for a couple of months, don't feel 'em any more. Strange ones always raise an itch. Funny that. Wonder if they get drunk biting Johnny, but probably they'll never bite him with me next to him, his blood is too bad. Always pick the richer blood they do ... And with this thought, which gives him a vague, comforting sense of pride, he too falls asleep.

Six enormous garbage cans filled to the gunnels stand piled on the edge of the pavement in front of the restaurant downstairs. They will be called for at 5:30 A.M. by the city health department. An enormous truck from which hefty men will jump. They swing up the full cans and, bang crash, with an incredible clatter, the empties are flung back to the pavement from the top of the truck. Takes skill to do that and make them land one next to the other and always right side up. A dog will have come first, then the rag and bone man with a stick will have grubbed out what he considers precious, later a rat or two and of course cats. Probably no hungry people, not just in this neighbour-hood; maybe, though. All these will have taken their little tribute from the six mute garbage cans, all in good order, before the skilful boys from the city health department come along carting it away and doing their little act of crash bang just where I wanted her - which never fails to give them joy. The sleepers upstairs never stir. They are used to noise.

On his way uptown (Johnny is still asleep, of course) Dick finds he is earlier than usual. All right, I want to see her. He takes it in his stride and never thinks about it. Want to see her, there it is. No reticence, no fool analysis, no dilly-dallying about why. He's had coffee for breakfast in a cafeteria, the thick soup-like brew has given him all the revitalizing energy he needs and he feels swell. He feels marvellous in fact, and everybody is his friend. Or rather everybody would be his friend if he saw anybody. As it is, he just grins like a friendly puppy and heads uptown. Down the subway and bang you are there, as though there were nothing in-between. Fact is, there is nothing in-be-tween, no on-the-way, because Dicky has seen nothing and felt not even the exuberant rush of the mob, because the mob, like himself, was each only trying to get someplace and that's all. A guy once fainted in the subway from hot air or lack of food or something and no one ever noticed it till someone, coming in, fell over him and ruined his hat. The hat made him sit up and take notice, looking around for somebody to sue. It's been down a hole on 14th Street for Dicky and out at 125th, up the street and here we are.

In the foyer you run the gauntlet of the doorman and the reception clerk, the bellboys and the elevator boy and, of course, the telephone girl. The whole place is run like a city in itself, entirely self-contained; you don't have to go out at all, everything you need is right there for you. Cinema downstairs, all the latest pictures, restaurant first floor, shops and chapel ground floor, get married, have your children baptised or confirmed if you feel like it, lectures Tuesdays and Fridays in the central hall for culture. Nursery school, tenants' advisory bureau, renting office, dentist, doctor and lawyer second floor. Pull your teeth for you, fix up your liver, collect your rent, psychoanalyze you, arrange your divorce. Art school third floor, and on top of it all, tier upon tier of self-contained apartments, eighty-six floors of them, all modern conveniences, bath with shower, running hot and cold water, central heating, kitchenette and combination bed and sitting room, $60 per month and dirt cheap, look at all you get. Swimming pool, gym and Turkish bath in the basement. Phone service free, you pay for each call, long distance is C.O.D., everything your little heart desires including electric refrigeration. The mob that watch over the foyer have a fine social sense, open doors only for the deserving and bow to people who realize that there is such a thing as Christmas. Nice people take off their hats in the lift when ladies come in. Dick has no hat. Betty lives in the house. She is there before him. It makes him feel good to see her. She's a swell looking girl. Pretty and a nice neat little figure, dark hair, full lips and soft they are, small firm breasts and slender ankles in high heeled shoes. Her eyelashes are black with mascara which makes them look long. Everything is just right. Nice dark eyes too, almond-shaped and slightly slanted and a retrousse nose. Jesus, she looks good, patting the clay with her slender hands, and he gives her a bright smile. "Hello, Betty." "Oh, hello," with a lilting intonation as though she hadn't seen him for ages and a slight twist of her body which says: how naughty you are. The two brief salutations convey all the playful intimacy of yesterday afternoon become today. But the brief sidelong glance with which she takes him in says: I know you. It is a warning which he does not get. This glance which she uses often is a camouflage, a flim-flam that she has unconsciously developed and retained because it is very effective and it covers her unrealized bewilderments. When something new comes along that doesn't fit right in with what she has all the answers for, something that has maybe given her a little shock - gee, what was that? - this look comes into her eyes all of itself. Usually it puts things right, gets it across to the other guy that she knows all about it and you can't fool her. And that was funny last evening, I didn't really mean to let him, just happened, couldn't help myself and I got a different sensation out of it. But Dick just doesn't get it. He continues to grin at her and walks over to help her adjust the armature for the little - clay statuette she is working on. She is trying to change the position of an arm and that involves bending the wire inside.

But when you bend the arm more the shoulder comes up higher, he tells her, and that swings out the hip and then the foot she's standing on comes in more, straight line from the ankle to the pit of the neck. "See?" Plumb line.

And deftly he does it. "Gee, that's right," she says with a sweep of her eyelashes upward and gliding over him. "Thanks," and in turning her hip touches him and their hands meet casually over the modeling tool. His fingers slide of themselves up the back of her hand and into the pit of her elbow - no one is looking - past her breast. "See you at lunch?" She nods, "Hm, hm," and he walks away to his own little clay figure which stands, wrapped in wet rags in the opposite corner. But the warning has been sounded. The experience of yesterday afternoon has not been so commentlessly engulfed and absorbed by her being as his easier thoughtlessness has permitted him to do. She is of a tougher fibre. No one can come along and burst into the nice rhythm of her dream. Not that way anyway, not out of the blue and without a by your leave. It isn't fair; she was only playing, just experimenting. She didn't mean anything by it, what's it all about? What goes on here anyway? And here he comes along and traps her. She'll fight.

He must have had hundreds of girls. Maybe ten, fifteen, maybe even thirty. Number thirty-one: me. How does she know? He just looks that way. Me, only Jack and Bill. Allan doesn't really count. Anything under two inches doesn't count. Highschool maxim. If anybody knew ... Of course Louise, she maybe suspects. I sort of confide in her. Must have somebody to tell. She's different, not like my sister at all. Bigger and older, so calm, but she misses things and for all that she's older she doesn't know that funny thing, that inside brooding thing, that sits in me and makes me have dreams with my eyes open. Dreams that are real and show me things as they really are, not just what they look like. All she thinks of is learning something, me, learn something, and I am learning, but in my own way, not the way she means at all. By seeing. And she can never understand the way things seem to me, that I am different, that I don't want the things everyone else is after, don't want money and success, to be anything, just want freedom and beauty. Her little lips curved in a slight smile, she thinks these two enormous words. She is unconscious of all the many generations that have epitomized their own nostalgic melancholia in the same terms. She is unconscious of the strident banality of these two words which are used each time the chasm between achievement and seeking, between wanting and desiring, doing and must-get-some-place, between progress and infinity needs stuffing up with some nice metaphoric cotton wool. Unconscious of the droning reiteration of these two words out of the mouths of politicians, kings, statesmen and the whole Punch and Judy galaxy of order and organization. They are new to her. Original. Her own discovery. That's it. I've got it. That's what I want. Freedom and beauty. She sees only their truth.

They are to her only the softer things in man. The sadder things for which there are no words. The selfless things. Her smiling lips express the lost seeking for what must be there. What has to be there, else how can we go on, even go on pretending. Freedom and beauty, the words for what is without substance and without form. The nebulous core, of the to be. Her lips go on smiling and pretty soon she begins to whistle softly between her teeth while she works. She is feeling pretty good. She got up early that morning, earlier even than her sister who goes to work. Up out of her warm soft bed and the sun was streaming in bright through the window. She had made breakfast for herself and her sister - tomato juice, a cereal with milk and coffee - and then she had sat for a long time trying out a new way to do her hair. Bangs? No, not bangs, too young looking. I'm grown up now and free. There ... sweep it over to the left behind the ear and long curls on the other side. A little bit like Sylvia Sidney; me, I look a little bit like Sylvia Sidney.[4] Better looking, that agent told me, when I thought I'd go on the stage, and then he tried to make me, but he was right. Careful with the mascara, hurts in my eye and, blinking, tears, smeared all over. There, done. Never use rouge, vulgar; much more interesting pale ivory, powder, but careful, my dress. A little powder had after all spilled on her dress. Easy enough to brush it off, but it makes the cloth shiny. She sat in front of the mirror looking at herself and a dab here and a pat, tuck in that stray bit of hair, never stays in place, with a little spit on my finger, looking at her eyes, how dark they are and long, and pretty soon her mind had drifted into her eyes and through and beyond them in the mirror into a gray haze, another world. In this lovely world there was no fixity, no norm. It was a limitless garden whose frontiers existed nowhere and could not be perceived by anyone outside. No one might seek her, seek to enter into the garden, because what happened within could not come from outside. What happened within was always creation and each day anew. It was creation of which she was the invariable center and nothing could exist in it if it were not placed there by her will. Nothing could obtrude. And it was an infinitely flexible world. A tree might mutate without transition into a mountain and the ocean into a quiet lily pond. A train rushing toward her while she struggled bound to the rails might all at once bear her within its royal coach.

Whether she entered it in gleaming armor at the head of a victorious army or drifted forlornly about in splendid loneliness set against a background of cypress and ruined marble temples, if she was the fettered victim on the altar of some lost antique ritual, the army, the cypress trees, the knife that hung over her in the hands of a priest were her own. Made by her, thought and seen by her. Inviolate. And yet it seemed as though an undertone whisper lay in her brain, as though her world were another life that she lived simultaneously with the other, harsher reality of now, as though the voice were her only true contact with this other being, giving form to that other life and making her its puppet. A hypnotic whisper translated into pictures through her eyes in the mirror.

But this morning the ringing of the telephone had soon interrupted her day dreaming. It was for Louise. Harold said to tell Louise he would call for her at 7 tonight. Of course, Harold had really been her boy friend at first, that is, she had met him first and taken him home and then he'd met Louise. Nearly every day he called now. Maybe Lou liked him? But the thought held little interest for her. She was going downstairs to work on her statue and she would make it really good. She was going to make a swell statue out of it and maybe some day have her own studio and make big things, life-sized and have exhibitions, though she cared little about that. She wanted to make beauty. Beauty was the keyword that opened the recesses of her secret being; the word was an Abacadabra of mystic personal import. A word that had meaning only when used tempo ingenio et modo, in the right manner, the right way and at the right time, and Dick had accidently stumbled on this six-letter magic combination.

That afternoon, after lunch, the second time they were alone together in her little room, she refused herself to him. It seemed to her that he was too casual, too sure, and it was revenge for the other acquiescence that had happened of itself. It gave her a momentary sense of superior amusement to lie next to him, allowing him to kiss her and when the kisses began to grow intense to withdraw, away from him, into herself. She said, "I am going home, soon, to Washington," deliberately irrelevant. But the ascendancy had eluded her. Somehow the words which she knew must follow: "Are you? Will you be back soon?" the "I wish you wouldn't go, I shall miss you," had given her no feeling of triumph by their comforting banality. That his response was as though read out of a book, the sitting up, the look into her eyes and taking her head in his hands - "I shall miss you" - that was familiar to her through experience and which she had expected, had missed fire. There was no joy in it. The game was meaningless. She thought, "but I am not going at all . . ." and sitting up she had said, "Well, maybe I won't go." He kissed her then, of course; but she would not be drawn back. They had begun to talk about art then - the interminable subject.

In the galaxy that constituted their fashionable Olympus, Picasso disputed the throne of Jove with Cezanne. Braque, Matisse, Klee, Brancusi, Van Gogh danced an erratic quadrille around these two, a quadrille of first position, second or third, while Gauguin held a stable outside position all his own. These gods were the barometer of their moods. While Picasso ruled their mood was harsh and vast, conceding nothing to human frailities, and if Cezanne stood before him it was gentler and in love with more tangible things. Only Gauguin remained with a constant undertone of romanticism because of course the South Sea islands were untouchable.

But soon their talk had drifted back to themselves.

"Are you always going to stay in New York?"

"Yes, I'm going to settle down here. I couldn't ever go back to Washington, the atmosphere stifles me. Here I feel free, it's so big."

Her eyes, dreamy, looked out over the gleaming river.

"It's big all right," he told her, "but it's tough too, I don't think you know how tough it is and heartless; nobody cares what happens to you and it isn't easy to be alone here."

"But that's what I like about it, don't you see? People are real here, living the way they want to live and not with everybody watching everyone else. Nobody bothers what you wear or who you are or anything."

"Yeah, well, they don't care if you starve either."

"Oh," she said with a little deprecating gesture, "I wouldn't care about that either."

"Not care?" he repeated, "Well baby, have you ever missed a meal?"

"But don't you see, it's all part of it; I want that too, I want everything. It's part of living, isn't it?"

But he did not see.

"It doesn't feel that way when you're hungry," he said, thinking of being cold in winter and without an over-coat and drinking water from the fountains in the parks to fill his belly so as not to feel it. All you think of is food. It takes you right out of yourself. All the other ideas go and disappear and you run around thinking how swell a bowl of soup would look to you, if I only had a dime, that place over there, I'd walk right inside and say, "One bowl of soup, buddy," to the guy behind the counter, "with three slices of bread and butter," and I'd sit down and eat it all up. With fifteen cents there'd be enough for coffee too. Eat it up and go out feeling good and even before it's finished maybe I'd think of a poem to write down or what a swell book that Tertium Organum by Ouspensky[5] is, begin thinking about awareness, and maybe some guy I know would come in or I'd go and see somebody and we could talk all night about awareness. But if I go to see anybody now it's to see if maybe they've got a dime to lend me so I can get something to eat. Gives you a headache too and maybe, if it gets real bad, cramps in the belly. You can stop them easy though by tightening your belt, real tight, or maybe drinking some water. Not the headache though, that keeps up for five or six hours, then you don't feel anything any more, not even awful hungry, just weak and sleepy. You lose your pride too, fast. If it's really bad you don't care how you get something into yourself. Guys you wouldn't talk to ordinarily, greet them with a bright smile, "Hello, Joe, got a cigarette? Thanks, say ... maybe you got a dime to lend me..." Being hungry, you waste so much time, walk miles maybe before something turns up, swallowing spit all the time and your mouth dries up inside and it feels as though your cheeks are slowly contracting inward. Look drawn and haggard. But the worst is all you think about is your belly. If I only had a dime, that place over there ...

These things are formlessly in his mind but she knows nothing of them. Her eyes are large and hurt.

"No," she says, "you don't see ... oh, you don't understand." Distress is in her voice. Understand. The word has been flung down. The implication is a betrayal and the duellist's challenge. You do not understand - the poor forlorn wail, the how we talk beyond each other, the heavy aloneness (will no one hear?). We are talking on different planes and what is there to do? The word is a withdrawal to which there is no reply. But Dick rose to the challenge. It was all a mistake, I must have knocked on the wrong door, I didn't know it was loaded, excuse me, but I meant the other Mr. Smith ...

His explanation performs magnificent gyrations and convolutions. He gesticulates and strides up and down. He gives a wonderful exhibition of circumlocution. And all because of the shock she has given him, the look in her eyes and the pain in her voice and the brisk punch in the solar plexus - you do not understand. Who? Me? Not understand? Of course I understand. Maybe I haven't made myself clear. It doesn't feel that way when you are hungry, but that doesn't mean that you aren't right. It just doesn't feel as though you are really living when you are actually starving; at least you don't think about anything worth while, and I don't know what you mean by living if it isn't something that really matters. But of course you are right because the experience is living too in a sense and maybe afterwards, when you are no longer hungry, you get something out of having been hungry. I just meant that it didn't feel that way at the time. See?

"Oh, well, yes, I see," she said, and she kissed him.

"You know, Betty," he said, looking down at her in his arms, "I think, I might fall in love with you."

They smiled at each other and were silent.

"Would you like me to be in love with you?"

She stirred in his arms and their lips came together softly and, for the first time, tenderly.

Louise came home from work at 6 o'clock, a tall dark girl, quiet and soft. Brushing off her little hat with one hand still closing the door she greeted them jauntily.

"Hello, children. Gee, I'm tired, must take off my shoes."

"Oh, Lou, Harold called up, said he'd be here at seven to take you out."

"Oh, I couldn't go out. Mr. Morton was so trying today, must have had a bad afternoon at golf yesterday or maybe in trouble with his wife."

Her low, dark voice kept up an interchange of little news with Betty's brighter one, but all the time her deep eyes were on Dick and her little sister, hiding an uneasy cynicism, a little disturbed question. The older sister. Dick felt uncomfortable. She knows me, he thinks, she suspects me and she doesn't like me. She probably thinks I'm dirty. Well, so I am, but what of it - bourgeoise. Open shirt, I hate neckties; don't care what she thinks. Let her suspect, none of her business; what is wrong with it anyhow? He is self-conscious and keeps interposing cigarette smoke between her and himself as a screen.

"Did you write home?" asks Louise, and Betty makes a little noise: "Oh, no, I forgot ... we were sitting here all afternoon talking," thus answering the half question in Louise's eyes.

"Well, you must have had a lot to talk about. . ."

"Oh, just things."

"We always have a lot to talk about," adds Dick, sardonic, getting a slap in both ways.

It is dismissed. Slyly Betty in a little pussycat way has taken care of everything with no more apparatus than an ingenuous intonation and a casual not even looking. Louise seems to relax. You couldn't really suspect little Betty, she is such a baby.

"Well, children," she says, "what are you going to do tonight?" Wants to be alone with Harold, sort of. I hope you are not going to hang around and spoil everything; it's really lovely outside. No, of course it isn't going to rain ,.. They look at each other: what are we going to do tonight? Dick, quicker on the uptake, says, "We were thinking of going to a movie. Let's have dinner some place Betty. O.K.?" "O.K.," she says and in ten minutes they are on their way. Waiting for the elevator to shoot up fifty-two floors he has to underline it. "Wants to be alone with Harold, I guess," he says, and Betty, with a little flirt of her shoulder meaningfully says, "Maybe."

Going out is a business that requires an elaborate mental readjustment which falls on her naturally and smoothly, like the coat she puts on. After the lipstick and tidy my hair, and a quick turn in the mirror (how do I look?), when the door shuts behind her, her face closes, becoming bland. The laxity of her posture drops away and she is taller, dignified, stately, neat, pretty, lady, woman. Her high-heeled shoes click firmly along the marble border of the hallway carpet. In the elevator she looks at no one, her eyes fixed unseeing to a rivet in the iron grating, counting the floors, 42, 37, 21, 15, 7 ... Ground Floor. In the foyer lurk the disillusioned attendants. They have seen them come and go. A grand duchess, complete with heralds and courtiers, would not impress them. Their judgment would remain strictly impartial, based on cash. Nothing for it but to walk precisely, step-by-step, heedlessly down the center carpet, her face unseeing and her body mute and unconscious, speaking no word to these slaves. But the street frees her. Her body relaxes and she dances by Dick's side, swinging her pocketbook, her mouth smiling, while her eyes flick here and there, eager and alert. That lovely car, ooh, a little bird, that man over there looking, and she takes Dick's arm.

"Are we really going to a movie?" she says. "Do you want to?"

"Oh, I don't know ..."

Too soon he says, "We could go to my studio ..." leaning toward her.

"I don't want to get home too late."

Battledore and Shuttlecock. Phrases off a phonograph record, back and forth, reaction a, b and c, all pat and neat. But it's a pleasant game of banter to them with a tiny little flick of a sting, just a slight and amusing tickle here and there to keep things alive.

"We can get there in ten minutes."

"Yes, but how long would we stay?"

They turn into a white-tiled restaurant and order the dinner (plat du jour), which, according to its taste and the claims of the management, has been cooked in a laboratory test-tube. Just so many calories, exactly what you need, vitamins x, y, z and q, plus one or two unknown ones perhaps, of course we don't claim that but well . . . Everything prepared under sterile conditions. But Dick knows better. He can smell the cockroaches in the soiled linen closet from where he is sitting. The walls are transparent to him. The chef, (heritage of la grande cuisine francaise, personal cook of the last of the Romanoffs, Leibkuechengerichterstatter Seiner Koeniglich und Kaiserlichen Majestat Friedrich der Grosse, Franz Joseph and what have you . . . that upstart Buonaparte had no palate worth speaking of) is a neurasthenic and flaunts his neurosis all over the kitchen range. The uppity waiters crawl into the kitchen, creep crawling on their slavering bellies, nice chef, pretty chefie, sweet chefie. They say, "Give us an order of porterhouse steak, chef, old boy." Tickle his balls for him - a nice porterhouse steak, red and juicy like your old jiggity juggety oomps, chefie. They do a little two-step, tip tap, pas de chat. A vicious clatter of pots and pans is their reward. A curse and a spit in the pan - Jesus Christ, leave me alone! - but it's a pro forma part of the necessary imbecile ceremony and they get their steak unburnt and unsullied, all laid out nice on a clean plate, and maybe a sprig of parsley and an extra potato, all nice on a nice clean plate, a platter washed by the dishwasher in his little cubbyhole just off the kitchen - turn to the left, gents, Mickey will wash 'em, over and over again. Mickey, the dishwasher, is a congenital idiot. In his little cubbyhole he stands, 6 x 9 feet it is with a deep sink on one side and a chute that opens in from the outside world to let in - krinkalang brump! - an unending stream of dishes, greasy and maybe still with a little bit of steak that Mickey snatches bovine glub-glub for himself without thinking. It's a one-way chute. In they come and Mickey washes them, standing on a ribbed board that allows the sloppingover to run down his apron, his pants, his cracked shoes, through the ribbing down the floor into a drainpipe hole in the middle of the floor. The sink is divided in half. On the left, soapy water and on the right, clean rinsing, and a little hand crane swivels agilely about from one to the other at Mickey's bidding, dipping a wire basket in which repose the dishes. First nice into one, up and down and up and down, Mickey's muscular arm dips and lifts them and swoosh, over to the other - there you are clean, let 'em drip to dry over the steam outlet and later sort cups and plates and saucers and salad plates and middle sizes and big dinner plates into nice even piles to be snatched away by the busboy[6] for redistribution and soon they'll be back. There's that one with the crack back again and Mickey the Greek seizes it and maybe sings, happy to have a job, tos pitimas andikron, mikro koritzu ... xanthomaloussa ... xanthomaloussamou orea, thinks Mickey, my beautiful blonde, and snatches a left-over olive off a greasy plate. The stone will keep him busy for a long time.

Karl, busboy Karl, feels the hole in his sock cut off the circulation in the big toe of his right foot inside the shoes without polish, without holeless soles, soulless holes, where the dust and the muck enters and coagulates. Hurts. And he goes down to the shithouse where he sits puffing half a butt while he changes right foot sock to left foot and left foot sock to right, folding under the circulation cutting hole. That's better - he wriggles his toes and sits a while reading contemplatively the inscriptions on the wall: Phone Columbus 1492 for a hot one ... Ask for Molly; and the cryptic diagrams: a triangle pierced by a cylinder from whose blunt end drop-squirt explosive drops; J. P., the lay of the land. He pricks up his ears, door opening, maybe the manager, better get out and going. Stink on his hands from the changing socks; quick, wipe on the bottom of his pants, he bursts out again into the bright-lit dining room. Yes, sir ... Grimly the manager swings his knout and Karl grabs quick a mop to slosh behind the footprints left by customers because it's raining outside.

Wong, yellow Chinkey Wong, the yellow Chinaman, the cellarman, the garbage man, sluggles around in pantoufles, collecting paper napkins and left-behind newspapers and odds and ends and bits and whatnots into largee bundle, collectee Wong pressee bale in pletty machine. He gathers slops and hoards them, his treasures, until his six garbage cans are full as full can be, and then he rolls them slowly, one by one, out into the area way, ready to be taken away, all lice and leat, and Wong, Son of Heaven, stands looking at the moon for a minute, the moon in the area way, thinking of Ming and Tong and Ting. Tonka Tunka Wong scratches his yellow scrotum and gets out his yellow whang. Wee wee Wong in the garbage cans.

Mary the Litvack has peeled all the potatoes and scraped all the carrots and turnips early in the morning. In the cellar she sat, a great basket full of the fruits of the earth between her solid thighs. Aye yai yai, she sang to each potato as it went scraped clean and naked, plunk into the bucket full of water by her side. Aye yai yai, and a little Russian song : Aye yai yai bublitschki ... Mary the Litvack, her great breasts slaggering with each scrape and scratch of the cunning knife, rrratch, a sliver of skin off the potato and the blade of the knife against the heel of her thumb. Like

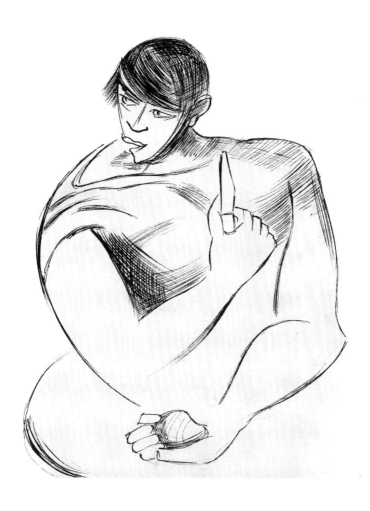

Mary the Litvack

tomcats there had come Karl and Mickey to purr around Mary and her great breasts.

"Aye, Mary, give us a feel." And a pinch they had at her behind that hung over a yard and a bit beyond the stool she sat on.

"Raack ..." screeched Mary, "Paskudnia!" And an air slash with the knife.

"Nice-a da Mary," says Mickey the Greek, grinning in a corner, xanthomaloussa muni.

"Nice-a da Mary," Karl apes him, "how you like geeve her leetle kitchy kitchy?"

And Wong, he too leedle fun grin grin, yellow from his own corner, thinks in Chinese: Nice-a da Mary the Litvack. The chef clatters with his pots and rattles his long shiny knives, shizz switt, against the whetstone to show that maybe some day he'll cut somebody's throat, because this is a hell of a job anyway and he'd be happy on a farm someplace with no one howling for fried eggs and bacon. He whistles a tune while the kitchen is empty:

"Te-ta-ta-ta-tee for a walking stick
For the girl he left behind him ..."

With a leer at the cashier who has come in for a cup of coffee. "Java? Try mine," he says.

Dick and Betty opposite each other at a small table gape out into the dining room's bright-lit sanitary glitter. Picking his teeth, that man all alone gazes clean through a wall, doesn't seem a bit absorbed in his incisors' little stringy bit of meat, really needs dental floss. Vacant, her eye passes him, sliding beyond to the frilly dress of that woman leaning, one hand poised with a smouldering cigarette, toward her escort: boy friend, fancy man, black shiny patent

leather hair all goo-oily brilliantine. Must leave greasy print
on the pillow where his head has been, maybe little volup-
tuous odor stays behind, Macassar oil and witch hazel,
Myrrh and Frankincense. Fat guy slopping down his food
with a paper by his side under his bilious eye and with a
blonde powderpuffing opposite him. My heart belongs to
Daddy, he'll get to her later. Coffee cups pushed aside, bits
of sugar demonstrate a new theory on the origin of motion
based on counteraction of gravitational pull while a zig-zag
version of the Brownian movement[7] grows, pencil drawn
on the table cloth, between four students. Bang go the
molecules, colliding all the time, crash, jig jiggety jogg jogg,
off in another direction, and that's at the bottom of it all. Do
they say "poddon me" somehow? Hen party given by nice
kindly ladies, enjoy their charlotte russe, eating with little
refined spoons, making delicate little passes at the whipped
cream. Fattening, but just this once. Where do they come
from? Away from hubby? Day a month out or school friend
reunion, once a year through thick and thin, sort of
d'Artagnan, now promise we'll meet all together just once
every single year no matter what may happen, or maybe
celebrating something, wedding, birth, funeral, or neigh-
borhood club for culture weekly session? Two boys from
the Elks' Club, drunk, flushed faces, lap down shot of whis-
key out of clandestine flask, tell smutty jokes, stop me if
you've ... here's a hot one. Lovers those two, boy and girl, no
more than eighteen, holding hands across the table, nice, all
eager faces and bright shiny eyes. Let go hands when waiter
goes by, embarrassed, silly, wish I too felt ... She turns
toward Dick whose bland preoccupied I-am-hungry look
becomes at once animated in response to her turning head.

"Look at those two over there."

"In love," says Dick heavily and gives Betty a melting look across the table before he too takes her hand. Her head sinks slowly, profile turning at a three-quarter angle toward her left shoulder, and it's a shepherd and shepherdess tableau, Meissen, Dresden, guaranteed best quality, with a little rose-shaded lamp standing on the table between. A little musicbox tinkle tinkles a minuet offstage. But blue smoke from the cigarette which he has quickly shifted to his left hand gets in between and in their eyes, making them glisten at first, but soon it begins to smart, and ash drops off the cigarette into a glass. It hisses. Hey, presto! The all-seeing eye of the manager has seen. It is his cue. Through a trapdoor in the floor he shoots up, surrounded by sulphur fumes and red magnesium flames. Black frock-coated, he stands by Dicky's chair. Imperviously his left hand beckons toward the back whence rush three waiters, while his right hand snatches the offending glass. "Excuse me, sir." He bends over the table and the tableau is destroyed. "Un autre verre! Vite!" he hisses at the menial; not his fault, the waiter's fault, the busboy's fault, act of God, glass shouldn't have been there. The other verre appears by a trick of legerdemain in his hand. Solicitously he sets it down, pats it, strokes it, shifts it a bit and disappears.

Thank you, says Dick to the empty air.

Their food now before them is quickly eaten, and over coffee they sit awhile, discussing what can we do now.

"Let's go and sit by the river."

"If we find a bench empty?"

In the tiny little park, four trees, a strip of grass and a slight serpentine of flag-paved roadway between two flights of cement stairs that lead down to it, there are four benches, one under each tree. Behind the trees a trellis covered with ivy hides the naked granite rocks on which the city stands. The green benches face the river.

The eye sees a glistening expanse of rippling water moving downstream and a wilderness of light running up the slope on the opposite shore. Strings of light that are roadways, moving lights that are automobile headlights, lights that go on and off that are windows in houses in which people live, gliding lights that are the eyes of little boats and a great magic composition of light which is an electric advertisement. It draws the eye which reads, fascinated and unbelieving, the moving script. At the top there is a great ball of fire from which emanate blue flashes of lightning. The lightning zigzags over the expanse of the sign and where it strikes words appear.

WRIGLEYS HERE
WRIGLEYS THERE
WRIGLEYS EVERYWHERE

and then a little gnome jumps up and runs, hippety-hop, skip jump, mechanically gay, over the top of the letters. When he reaches the end of his run the miracle disappears. The sign flashes out, but not for long. Soon there appears a golden band along which flicker dark letters that spell out other words.

THE TIME IS NOW EXACTLY 9:45 P.M.

and with the appearance of the cypher the running band becomes still. The numerals remain alone, precisely in the center.

9:45 P.M.

But very soon the ball of fire is born again at the top of the sign and its blue flashes of lightning spell again the omnipresence of Wrigleys until:

THE TIME IS NOW EXACTLY 9:46 P.M.

No one has thought to add a little epicene Tempus Fugit. There is no comment. That's how it is and that's all there is to it. Even the more spectacular reiteration of the all-presence of Wrigleys is no more than a commentless statement of blunt fact. But the foliage of the four trees whispers above the benches. A little bit of the moon glistens in broken bits of silver on the river and a vast star-glittering sky curves deep overhead. Dick and Betty are silent. The river makes a little lapping sound as it flows swiftly past, eager to lose itself in the sea, and this sound is hypnotic. It takes hold of their brains and soothes them. This little sound becomes a humming murmuring, weaving lace designs in their brain, taking hold of them, soothing thought and desire slowly out and away and under, sinking softly into an awesome silence like the green bottom of the sea in which they are alone.

Her head, upturned, leans back, eyes closed, embraced by his left hand around her shoulder, he bent over her, kissing soft warm moist slowly unfolding lips, his right hand touching caressing, gripping the yielding pulsing flesh of her arm, wrist, pressing, turning against the supple slow rising breast. Again and again, wordless, to sink, slipcurling inward, down into the dark and silent sense, this calm absorption; to rise again, feeling secure, safe in this small thing, you and I. From the bottom of the sea, quiet to rise again, slowly dropping petals, the lips still gently clinging fall apart, with the sweet taste of her breath soft in his mouth.

THE TIME IS NOW -

Again to seize, avid, to lose, again to seize, to find, uncomprehending, the warm wombsense of these kisses, absorbed, now backward to sink a golden glow of darkness, slipping again over the stirring mind. Alone in a strange past world, encased protected inside a bell of glass.

Crunching steps on the cement stairs awaken and separate them. Their eyes, glistening and softened, look out over the river again, colliding at once against the noisy brilliance of THE TIME IS NOW ... back to seek the moment destroyed by steps on those stairs; into the mind had flashed the vague apprehension: must not be seen. The trees whisper loudly in a cold wind and, shivering, they feel a passing vision of fearfulness and alone.

10:32 P.M.

What is this thing that is happening to me? Cars squeal, (brakes) hoot an impervious out-of-the-way, turning corners in the streets behind the trees.

"I must go now," she says, offering her lips again.

"I love you Betty," the words lost in her breath. He kisses her again.

"What do you say now, Betty?" he says, hardly knowing his own meaning.

She makes a little sound and turns her head against his shoulder. She has nothing to say. No statement to make; Madame cannot see reporters today. Both are bewildered, this is not their plan at all. Their drift has been toward a brave new freedom, an esoteric aloneness in which they hung suspended as the central deity whose sense was law, not responsible - the king can do no wrong - and here this thing has come along, this thing love, the flowery chains, and established a current between them which they cannot resist. Love, the word that is too strong for them, that they dare not resist, fearful of offending the tradition of man.

"It'll be all right," he prattles, "we'll be all right. We'll work together and help each other and I can show you so many things."

Vaguely his hand waves in the air, the conjuror's hand, ladies and gentlemen, it's the ace of hearts, quicker than the eye ... Dressed in the star-studded mantle of the master necromancer, he stands before her. His right hand holds extended in an impervious gesture the magic wand shining with the symbols of Isis and of Arriman, on his shoulder sits scratching its bald head a raven, companion of Wotan and bird of all wisdom. He stands within the mystic circle around which are inscribed the names of Hebrew archangels: Ariel, Uriel ... the signs for eternity and for the more tangible eternity whose sign is a triangle: alpha, omega ... Around his feet purrs an immense black cat, her yellow eyes spitting fire. He waves his wand and mountains arise on the horizon. I give you these. His wand waves again and streams of gold flow down before her feet. The skies split and cover her with roses, deer come to lick her hands, lions to crouch at her feet, doves flutter past and kiss in passing her lips with their tiny rosy beaks. An immense Rolls Royce car, bearing her royal crest, rolls up noiselessly: for her. They are on the deck of a Spanish galleon, dressed in velvet and lace, captain of the pirates, conqueror of the Indies. A magic castle opens its portals for her, the floor is paved with gold and the pillars are ruby. In an idyllic valley, shut off from the world, they live as Amor and Psyche. For a moment he is gigantic and strong.

"It'll be all right, we'll be all right." He holds her in his arms.

"I have never felt this way before," she says.

"Do you love me?" he asks the question that is a confession of uncertainty, or an arrogance. She does not answer.

"Do you?"

"I don't know," says her small voice, and something seems to collapse within him.

The necromancer is transmuted into a small child in swaddling clothes. Drooling, cooing, lala, mama, tome tiss me, it smiles appealingly, round blue eyes large and hurt in its tiny-tot face.

"I'd do anything for you, if only you love me."

She kisses him again, softly now, deliberately and cool. It is in her thoughts that this has been a nice evening. He is nice. She likes him, maybe she does love him; he is so sensitive. Tonight she will lie awake and think about him, dreaming, reliving the strangeness that has come to her and which she fears. Content with her kiss, his buoyant spirits rise at once. How sweet she is. They walk slowly toward her house hand in hand and not speaking at all.

"Goodnight, Betty, see you tomorrow."

"Yes, tomorrow, I'll be down early."

With a last little flirting smile she is gone in through the revolving doors.

He returns alone to the little park and sits on the same bench trying to recapture the feeling of this evening.

11: 09 P.M

The moon is gone. The water bubbles past more swiftly now on the outgoing tide and, unlit, it is sallow gray and hard,

all surface and a little sinister, carrying bits of waste, bob-
bing along, twistturning, an empty half-shattered egg crate,
bits of paper, flat open newspaper sheets, limp and untidy.
Dick cannot keep his agile mind on the romantic impulse
that sent him back to this bench. His mind whirls with the
current in little eddies, circling round and around the central point - she - and off in long, unexpected streamers. Like
sinking into a warm sort of darkness and away out of
myself, as though the kiss, no, the act, had become all I.
Nice, she, easy to hold with her little cat way, soft, seems to
slip into my arms easy without effort, all supple, giving her
whole warmth. Eyes close of themselves and like pulling
slowly a blanket over the brain. Strange how it is akin to
death. Death. What if I were to jump into this river, floating
down with the tide, sink into the sea? Fish come and eat me,
sharp needle teeth, probably get caught in the propellor of
some ship, cut to bits, gory mess, crunching cracking bones.
Long ago since I broke my leg, femur multiple fracture,
healed good though, only feel pain now when the weather
changes. Lying stiff on my back, up to the hip packed tight
in plaster with weights on the foot to keep it straight and
anaesthetic twice, clapping a rubber mask over my face
from behind and telling me to count slow and holding my
breath. It is like looking through the wrong end of a telescope and a thing way off in the distance begins to hum,
whirling faster and faster, louder and louder, always toward me, always faster and louder, the hum rising to a
screech like trains on rails in curves, and always faster,
nearer through the telescope until with an unbearable high
loud sound it passed into me and I was out. Then they can
do what they like, cut you to bits and you wouldn't feel it.

A half-shattered egg crate.

If you died you wouldn't know it. Maybe though there is such a thing as waking up dead. It can't just finish, all end in nothing ...

A childhood memory floats back to him. Being ill and in delirium, the hot fever lying heavily on him and making him feel the enormous weight of each limb and his body, he had all at once woken up dead. He had awakened feeling free and light, endowed with the power of moving effortlessly through the air. He had floated away from his body, delighting in the strangeness of this ease, toward the ceiling of the room, passing through the ceiling into an otherworldly and somehow clearer sphere. Looking back, he had seen from an immense height his body lying on its couch and a vision came to him of his mother and his sister kneeling by the couch and weeping. He had been able to look into their senses and into their future and within the inner being of his mother he had seen the collapse of a dream. He had been able to see that she would look upon her life as empty and purposeless because of his death. Cooly he had seen this and an esoteric thought process that was not thought but understanding had at once given him the comprehension that not out of compassion for her but because it did not matter to him, because he would lose nothing, he would return, and with that understanding he had been back in his body on the bed, calling it a fever dream. A fever dream that he could not now distinguish from reality. Like the heavy dream visions of childhood, puberty. What if they were real, these things that come to torture the child at night? Two years of fearing the night, fearing the dark, and sensing sleep as a dark enemy from the nether world. Fearing to close staring eyes lest there

Fearing the night.

come again a gigantic gnarled tree-branch hand, filling the room to strangle the child, lest there come to sit by the bed to watch and creep and leer three silent figures with evil eyes, lest a clammy, formless thing lay itself again, pressing heavier and heavier over the heart and mouth and the face, engulfing slowly, slowly, all the body, vampires come to suck the blood and green rats to gnaw the toes, a thing to stand in the corner, stand and stare motionless all night long exuding a force - you must look, you must look, you cannot turn your head, you cannot turn away, you cannot move, you cannot close your eyes. Agonized the child struggles to turn away to move - if I could move my hand, if I could even move one single finger the spell would be broken - but the weight holds, holds fast and tight and heavy and nothing moves except the racing heart until sleep comes through exhaustion. What if these things were real? Too easy, too facile, the suave soothing explanations of psychology. Old wives' tales picked up from naughty maids and unwise mothers, the bogeyman will get you if you don't look out, in the too literal imagination of the child. Blow on it and make it well, pat on the back, find a good tangible reason and that explains it - as though a reason were an explanation. Bang goes the lightning and all the women and children scream, even strong men tremble, savages howl and crouch, their snouts pressed into the ground, peasants say: mustn't look, because if you do you'll see the sky split with the flash and get a look straight into heaven. Then you'll go blind because God doesn't like nasty peeping Toms, prying Harrys, wants you to respect his privacy. Chinese beat drums and set off firecrackers. Worse an eclipse, convinced dragon has come to swallow the sun, rush around something fearful, praying and screaming, beating pots and gongs, even the beasts in the field lowing: moo moo, behuuu, joggle away to the nearest fence in a panic, hang their long faces over and stare, slupping with meaty wet tongues bits of snot off their noses. In walks a wise old owl, furled umbrella, red flannel underwear, thick bottle-glass lenses to hide his red-veined, puss-yellow eyeballs, and glittering ferret pinpoint retina, sloppy beard, tobacco and soup stained, and no good he is in bed. Says, "There there now, pish tush, it's all right, it's simple, just ask me." Lightning, i.e. discharge of static electricity. Eclipse, i.e. given juxtaposition of the earth, moon and sun at rare intervals when their elipses coincide. Goggle goggle go the women and children sucking their thumbs. The strong men rally round, back patting, sure, of course, what'd I tell you, knew it all the time, nothing to it and in chorus they reiterate a lilting magic chant: discharge of static ellellithithy. Old owl gives them cold stares and spits in their faces. Superiority of pure intellect. Only the Chinese still go on beating gongs and kettledrums. Quaint old custom.

Walking down that country lane alone late at night, dark black it was and the trees whispering to each other jeering threats at me. A dozen times I shied from tall tree men forms, gnarled and creaking, waving their many-fingered hands, reaching for me to grip, following behind, mustn't turn to look. Lot's wife. Dry creaky voices.

Carved your initials into my bark with a knife, hack me down for firewood to burn and crackle, twisting agony, to warm your bones. Climbing up into my branches after birds' nests, my guests, scraping the bark with heavy shoes and a shameful exhibition: pissing from the top branch to see could you hit the stone on the ground. Into the faces of my sisters, Daphne, Chloe, green they blushed.

Nightbirds had wailed their unhappy call: Eeeeeekuhoo, moulting feather smell in the air. Strangler, murderer, our children, our sorrow, our pain. The naked bird children, broken necks popping shoe-button eyes, porous skin tinted saffron, green and putrefaction yellow peep-caw open-beaked out of the grass. "Keepacaw, kee," he had heard their cawk, their corpse cry back to reproach him. Perhaps they too lived on somehow to wait for him, for revenge.

Bows and arrows carved out of my flesh for shooting at cats, poor tabby toms crying their love to the stars. Two arms of mine to get the fork for a catapult. Four years to grow them and now they are charred stumps.

Do trees feel? Does a lettuce leaf quail each time you bite into it? Do flowers weep in pain when you pick them?

What do we know of the many forms of consciousness that must exist alongside our own, the heartbeat of a boulder, the dreams of insects and of beasts, perhaps the sea itself has thought and feeling of a kind unapproachable to us. We trample heedlessly over the world, cunning parasites, naked pink bodies inside our ridiculous clothes. The beasts have no souls to us and the stones no senses, the plants no feeling. They do not know pain, we say, as though pain must necessarily be a telegraph system of nerves, as though perception could not exist except through a steaming pudding, veined and quivering: the brain. What do we know even of each other? What do I know of Betty except what she is to me. I cannot be one with her, see into her, except without thought, and then I, her, and I in her, I lose myself. Lose myself and forget to watch and to see, forget to know until, coming back, at once a great rift comes between us. My thoughts turn away and do not hold her at all. How alone we are. Moodily he lights a cigarette and watches the drifting bits of waste float past. The waste meets, bumps and separates again. The water gives it a gurgling, preoccupied, busy little voice. The voice says, "Me, me, me, me, me . . ."

Like Lunar night-moths attracted by the light of his cigarette, two bulky policemen descend the steps slowly, loping sliding step of the cunning hunting wolf, and range themselves before him.

"Ain't you got no home?" one.

"Whaddaya doing here anyway?" two.

"Don't you know it's late?" the first.

"Just sitting here thinking, officer," apologetic, anxious jitters, grinning, Dicky, fluttering as carefree and elegant a hand as ever was fluttered.

"Thinking?" the first, enormous scorn in his voice.

"Yeah?" the second, "you better do your thinking at home."

"G'wan, beat it now, buddy," the first.

Carefully bridling, trying to save his face, "Why, anything wrong with it? Can't I sit here? What's the time anyhow?" asks Dicky, hurt voice and grinning brotherhood, just one of the boys.

"1:30. See?" says number one, "ain't you got no eyes?" his arm points across the river, the arm of Nemesis.

"Yeah, no time to be thinking," says number two.

Motionless, two dark archaic forms, they watch him climb the stairs. Stepping deliberate and slow he walks step by step, not to be hurried; I have nothing to be afraid of, they can't do anything to me, up the stairs, stopping at the top to light carefully another cigarette. Show they can't push me around.

"Screwball," says archaic form number one.

"Thinking," snorts two, "like as not he was diddling himself. Caught a couple here the other day, right behind this same bench, right here lying flat on the grass, jumping up and down so hot they never heard me come up to them. Nice piece the broad was too, wouldn't have minded giving her a good going over myself. So she starts to blubber and whine: `Please, officer, you ain't gonna arrest us,' and all the time the guy has the shakes so bad he can't get his pants buttoned. I could have bust out laughing. I let 'em go in the end."

"Slip you something?" asks his shadow.

"Five."

"Could have got ten out of 'em."

"Don't think they had it."

"The things you see on this beat," he muses, "two, three weeks ago, 'round three in the morning I'm walking along a little further down and I was just thinking I'll maybe knock off for a while and get me a sandwich around the corner when somebody lets out a scream down by the river, just one yip. First I think its maybe cats but anyway I think I better have a look and I head for it. When I get there I can't see nothing so I beat the bushes around and be Jasus if I don't find a couple of fairies crouching in a hedge. Stark naked one of them was and the other without his pants. I

The Perverts

kicked them into their clothes and took 'em down and charged 'em. All the way down to the station they was hollering and squealing like guinea pigs to let 'em go." He apes a sissy voice, " `Please officer, we'll do anything for you.' Well, I get 'em in and the Sergeant says, `What's the charge?' and when I tell him he gets red in the face and nearly jumps through the ceiling. `Fairies,' he says to 'em, `dirty filthy buggers, if I had my way they'd take you and cut your lousy stinking balls off. Like to do it myself. Take 'em out of my sight.' he hollers at me. `Put 'em downstairs and put 'em in separate cells, the dirty stinking filthy bastards.' Couldn't charge 'em with nothing but indecent exposure, though. To get 'em good you have to catch 'em in the act and there has to be two witnesses. They would have got two years if we could have got 'em proper. On the indecent exposure they got three months each. Judge looks at them like they was dirt."

The other noisily sucks snot through his nose into his mouth and spits it out into the grass.

"Ain't nothin' like a park beat for stuff like that," he says, "kick their tails good for them, I would, if I was to catch them at it, fucking perverts."

His virile bull voice is filled with vicious hate. They move on, ferret eyes gleaming, alert and eager, peering into the bushes and behind benches, padding softly on their feet, tracking, scenting, sniffing, questing to find sexual evil, to root it out, destroy it, grind it into the dust, to wallow in the blood of perverts, rip out their entrails, cut out their hearts and fling their torn organs into the gutter, food for dogs and rats.

Crouching on a tall stool, feet drawn up, elbow on the marble top counter, his hand abstractedly scratching dandruff and grease on his scalp Dick gapes vacantly into a mirror watching himself suck malted milk through a straw. Sleepily, bovine eyes staring blank into the empty street, the night man, wipes again and again, rub, rubbing with a limp gray cloth the same spot behind the coffee urn, where it is warm. Peeeee, whistles thinly the shiny coffee urn: peeeeeeeeeeeeeeee.

Appendix

Speakeasies were illegal drinking establishments in America during Prohibition. The term comes from a patron's manner of ordering alcohol - a bartender would tell a patron to be quiet and 'speak easy.'

Speakeasies were formed in the 1920's as a means to get around the everyday hassle of law enforcement watching for people to violate the 18th Amendment. As a result of Prohibition, the speakeasy was an established institution. For every legitimate saloon that closed as a result of the new law, a half dozen underground palaces sprung up. These speakeasies were one of the many ways that people during the 1920's and early 1930's obtained illegal alcohol. By the middle of the decade there were thought to be 100,000 speakeasies in New York City alone. Patrons often said you could get a glass of liquor at any building on 52nd Street between Fifth and Sixth Avenues in New York City ... if you knew where the speakeasies were and if you had the password to get in. [From Wikipedia.]

1. Apollonic and Dionysian: A reference to The Birth of Tragedy by the philosopher Nietzsche in which he discusses the history of Greek tragedy, and introduces a dichotomy between the Dionysian and Apollonian, seen on the one hand as representing emotion and sensation, and on the other reason and cognitive thought.

2. John B. Watson was an American psychologist who established the psychological school of behaviorism. In 1913 Watson published an article which was to be seen as 'The

Behaviourist Manifesto'. In it he writes 'Psychology as the behaviorist views it is a purely objective experimental branch of natural science. The behaviorist, in his efforts to get a unitary scheme of animal response, recognizes no dividing line between man and brute.' With his behaviorism, Watson put the emphasis on external behaviour of people and their reactions to given situations, rather than the internal, mental state of those people. In his opinion, the analysis of behaviours and reactions was the only objective method to get insight in the human actions.

3. Vachal Lindsay was an American poet. In the text Heinz is probably referring to Lindsays poem 'The Congo' which has been described as racist. At the time it was published in 1912 Lindsay was widely seen as an allay of blacks as a result of this poem and others.

4. Sylvia Sidney was born in the Bronx in New York in 1910. She became an actress at the age of 15 and in 1926 was spotted by a Hollywood talent scout. During the great depression Sidney made many films often playing the girlfriend or sister of a gangster including An American Tragedy and You Only Live Once.

5. Tertium Organum by the mystical Russian philosopher Ouspensky is presented by him as the 'third instrument of thought' after Aristotle and Bacon. In the book he uses the concept of the fourth dimension as an extended metaphor for the esoteric nature of reality, starting with the question 'What do we know and what do we not know'? Tertium Organum was published in America in 1922.

6. A Busboy is an assistant in a restaurant principally responsible for setting and clearing tables. The busboy also typically serves drinks and sweeps up.

7. Brownian motion describes the phenomenon of minute particles immersed in fluid following random zig-zag paths. The motion is caused by molecules in the fluid bumping in to the particles they encounter. If these are sufficiently small they will be bounced into motion and will abruptly change trajectory as they are hit by further molecules.

Bibliography

New Directions in Prose and Poetry No 14. New Directions 1953 New York. Anthology including the original publication of *The First Thing.*

Heinz Henghes. *A Phase of the European Dilemma.* The Adelphi. June 1939

Joan Wyndham. *Love Lessons: A wartime diary.* Virago Press 2001 ISBN 1 86049 877 9 First published by William Heinemann Ltd in 1985

Paul R. Bartop and Gabrielle Eisen. *The Dunera Affair - A documentary resource book.* Schwartz & Wilkinson and the Jewish Museum of Australia 1990. ISBN 1 86337 025 0

Cyril Pearl *The Dunera Scandal.* Angus & Robertson 1983. ISBN 0 207 14707 8

K.G. Loewald *A Dunera internee at Hay 1940-41.* Historical Studies Vol 17 No 69 Oct 1977. University of Melbourne

Anais Nin *Nearer The Moon the unexpurgated diary of Anais Nin 1937-1939.* Peter Owen 2003. ISBN 0 720 61206 3

Kay Sage. *China Eggs.* Bilingual English / French edition translated into French by Elizabeth Manuel. Starbooks / Editions de l'Etoile. Charlotte, Seattle 1996.
ISBN 0 9645677 2 5

Heinz Henghes, Retrospective exhibition of sculpture and works on paper, England & Co 2006, ISBN 1 902046 35 8

An online catalogue of works, a chronology and various articles and resources are available at: **www.henghes.org**

Additional links relating to this book are at: **www.henghes.org/ecceego**